VOCABULARY REPAIR KIT

ANGELA BURT
WILLIAM VANDYCK

Illustrated by David Farris

*Hodder
Children's
Books*

a division of Hachette Children's Books

Text copyright © 2002 Angela Burt and William Vandyck
Illustrations copyright © 2002 David Farris

Editorial by Gill Munton
Design by Joy Mutter

Cover illustration by Mark Oliver

First published by Hodder Children's Books in 2002
This edition published in 2006

ISBN: 978 0 340 91834 0

A Catalogue record for this book is available from the
British Library.

Printed in the UK by CPI Bookmarque, Croydon, CR0 4TD

Hodder Children's Books
A division of Hachette Children's Books
338 Euston Road, London NW1 3BH
An Hachette Livre UK company

CONTENTS

INTRODUCTION

Oi!

Not much of a word, is it?
Some people would even say that it isn't a word at all.

But they're wrong, so we can forget about them – ha!

Or can we? At first sight, it doesn't seem to be much of a word.
For a start, it's only two letters long. It hasn't even got any
consonants in it. It doesn't have a very "clever" feel, does it?
But just hold on a second. Have a closer look.

Oi!

Not at the letters, fool.

The thing is, it's only two letters long, but it'S STILL REALLY GOOD.
Look what it can do.

Used in the right way, it really grabs the attention, doesn't it?
It makes you think: "What's going on? Am I in trouble, or about
to do something which someone else doesn't think is right?"
The alarm bells go off, don't they? Used in the right way at the
right time, it beats the pants off "Excuse me, I don't want to be
a bother, but I wonder if I could possibly trouble you for just a
momentito of time ..."

Used in the right way, at the right time, **oi** is really arresting.

And that's one of the great things about words. Used in the right
way, they can make things happen. If you've read this far, you're
probably quite clever (and, frankly, good-looking). But it's not about
being clever. If you can use the right words at the right time, you
will probably go a long way. Sure, you'll be able to pass exams,
get a job, etc. etc. But you'll be able to make an impact. You'll be
able to persuade people to do things. Make them like you, want
to give you things. You'll be able to make people feel better, or, if
you like (let's say they've really asked for it), make them feel awful.
You will have a power over people.

And if you don't believe it, just think about all the people you
know. Think of the ones who are good at using words. They've got
something worth having, haven't they?

But you've got to know how to use words. And here is the first lesson.

Oi! Don't overuse words. You see, a word loses its impact if you use it too often. That last **oi**, for example. Didn't make such an impact as the first one, did it? No. Hmm. What if someone you know went round saying "oi" the whole time? After a while, that person wouldn't be surprising, or arresting, or attention-grabbing, would they? They'd just be the person who said "oi" a lot. A bit boring, really. No, it was the freshness of the first **oi** that made it work, wasn't it?

So the more words you know, the better. You'll have plenty of fresh ones to choose from. Knowing more words will also mean that you have a greater chance of being able to use one that's just right. One that hits the nail on the head.

LESSON 2

Unfortunately, it's time for a small amount of bad news.

The fact is that words are **useless**

... er ... if you don't know how to use them.

For example, spelling is important:

The pealing of the bells   **The peeling of the bells**

INTRODUCTION

There's a lot of scope for giving the wrong impression of things by using a word that is not quite the right one. For example, if you wrote in a thank-you letter: "You must be telepathic!", that would be nice. It would suggest that the person has bought you exactly what you wanted. It's a nice way of saying that you're grateful. It paints this sort of picture:

Person getting present

Happy expression

Person giving present

However, if you wrote, "You must be psychopathic!", that would be rather different.

You'll need some help, then.

Here's Zelda.

Here's Colin.

And there's Steven.

So, let's go. And don't forget: we don't promise you the usual rubbish. We promise you

THE WOR(L)D!

WORD ROOTS

Many of the words we use today are based on Ancient Greek or Latin words.

For example, **aquarium**, **aquatic**, **aqualung** and **aqueduct** all come from the Latin word for water (**aqua**).

Yeah, yeah, that's great to know. I mean, really. In no sense am I just sitting here thinking: SO WHAT?

Well, the fact is interesting in itself.

WORD ROOTS

OK, OK. There is another reason. Knowing one word can help you to understand and spell loads of others. For example, once you know **cent** is Latin for **100**, you will be able to understand:

- why 100ths of a metre are called **centimetres**
- why 100 cricket runs are called a **century**
- why there are 100 **cents** in a dollar

This means that:

- you'll remember how many centimetres there are in a metre
- you'll know how to spell the word **centimetres** and that it is **dollars** and **cents**, not **sents**

The words below are all derived from the Latin word (**pes, pedis**) for **foot**. Look at the clues and complete the words.

1. ped _e_ _l_   a lever you work with your foot
2. ped _ _ _ _ _ _ _ _   a person who walks
3. ped _i_ _c_ _u_ _r_ _e_   care of the feet and toenails

Using your new-found knowledge, how would you spell the name of the creature which has lots of feet?

4. sentypeed __   sentipede __   centipede __

The Ancient Greek word for **time** is **khronos**. Give the meaning of each of these words:

5. chronological _____

_____

6. synchronise _____

_____

7. chronic _____

_____

To get things into chronological order, Zelda took out her chronometer to time the synchronised swimmers. It was then that she realised that they were chronically silly.

8. So, come on then, can you work out what a **chronometer** is?

_____

Three of these words are derived from the Latin word (**legere**) meaning **to read**. Which ones, and what do they mean?

9. legible _____

10. lectern _____

11. lecture _____

12. delectable _____

13. Show the connection between the meaning of the word **hypothermia** and the Greek word **therma** meaning **heat**.

DICTIONARY SEARCH (1)

In all these words, **escent** means **becoming**. Becoming ... WHAT? Make this clear in your definition of each word. The first one has been mucked up for you.

1. adol**escent** _____

Becoming a doll?

That's SO immature.

2. conval**escent** _____

3. efferv**escent** _____

4. obsol**escent** _____

5. putr**escent** _____

DICTIONARY SEARCH (2)

In each box, try to write at least three words that have the Greek or Latin root word somewhere in them. Make sure that the root word relates to the meaning of the words you write.

tech (Greek: **skill**)	**nov** (Latin: **new**)
dyna (Greek: **power**)	**magn** (Latin: **great**)

NOVAMAGNADYNA TECHROD
the Best Drain Rods
EVER

BORROWED WORDS

Why is there no ham in a hamburger?

Many English words have been taken from other languages. We sometimes change the spelling slightly – and we sometimes leave it as it is.

Here are just a few examples.

confetti	Italian: means **little sweets traditionally thrown at weddings**
hamburger	German: means **originating from the city of Hamburg**
poodle	German (pudeln): means **to splash in water**
biscuit	Latin (bis coctus): means **twice cooked**
denim	French (serge de Nîmes): means **from Nîmes**, where the fabric was made
bungalow	Hindi (bangla): means **belonging to Bengal**, where there were lots of single-storey houses
malaria	Italian (mal'aria): means **bad air**; it was once thought that malaria came from marshy, foul-smelling places
kimono	Japanese: means **something to wear**

So now you can tell Mr Clevertrousers why there's no ham in a hamburger (before you hit him).

I don't need foreign words for a **pukka** night out: I just go for a good old British **curry** and **lager**, and then I come back to my **bungalow** and get into my **pyjamas**.

A dictionary would be useful for the next activity. If you don't have one, just guess, and then look up the answers in the back of the book.

FOOD AND DRINK

Find out which language each of these words comes from.

1. spaghetti _____

2. sugar _____

3. gateau _____

4. chutney _____

5. kebab _____

6. omelette _____

7. vodka _____

We've taken food words from all over the world. Think of tiramisu, coleslaw, quiche, pasta, moussaka, enchilada ...

Mmm, this is what I call learning.

17

WORD SEARCH

Use all the clues to work out these words and to find them in the square. A word may be arranged vertically, horizontally or diagonally, and may be written forwards or backwards. The same letter may be used more than once.

c	n	p	e	f	a	c	k	w
o	o	q	x	t	u	s	i	i
u	o	u	u	r	r	z	p	g
r	v	m	r	e	o	b	o	w
g	l	y	w	g	y	e	l	a
e	r	o	c	n	e	f	o	m
t	b	g	a	d	g	t	h	j
t	c	a	s	i	e	s	t	a
e	b	r	o	c	h	u	r	e

Meaning	Language of origin	Word
1. a young marrow	French	c _ _ _ _ _ _ _ _
2. a spicy Indian dish	Tamil	c _ _ _ _
3. an illustrated information booklet	French	b _ _ _ _ _ _ _
4. a system of relaxing exercises	Sanskrit	y _ _ _

5. a small restaurant
   selling snacks   French   c _ _ _

6. hockey on
   horseback   Balti   p _ _ _

7. a tent made   N. American Indian   w _ _ _ _ _
   from skins

8. an afternoon nap   Spanish   s _ _ _ _ _

9. a repeat piece of
   music as requested   French   e _ _ _ _ _

10. a woodwind   French   o _ _ _
    instrument

FOREIGN PHRASES

What do these mean?

1. cul-de-sac   _____

2. en suite (bathroom)   _____

3. per annum   _____

4. au pair   _____

5. vice versa   _____

6. R.S.V.P.

   (Répondez s'il vous plaît.)   _____

WHAT AM I?

Use the clues to help you to work out these words.

1. el lagarto (Spanish)   a large reptile like a crocodile

— — — — — — — — —

2. campo (Hindi)   liquid soap for washing
your hair

— — — — — — —

3. robota (Czech)   a machine that can do work
normally done by humans

— — — — —

4. zarafah (Arabic)   the tallest animal in the world

— — — — — — —

5. kaki (Urdu)   the yellowish-brown colour used for
Army uniforms

— — — — —

6. bangli (Hindi)   a bracelet

— — — — — —

OVERUSED WORDS

We use words like **nice**, **good**, **wonderful**, **bad**, **boring** and **awful** so often that they've become very vague in meaning, and rather tired. After all, why use the same words all the time?

First of all, it's a bit dull.

Secondly, you may not get quite the right shade of meaning.

So, if you have a wide vocabulary, your writing will be fresh and precise in meaning.

Choose your words carefully if you want to say what you mean.

OVER TO YOU

Use the words in the box to describe a best friend, a top musician and a good meal. Use each word once only.

honest	tasty
talented	entertaining
thoughtful	kind
tuneful	appetising
delicious	helpful
rhythmic	satisfying

1. A best friend is _____ _____ _____ _____

2. A top musician is _____ _____ _____ _____

3. A good meal is _____ _____ _____ _____

BANNED FOR UTTER DULLNESS AND IRRITATING REPETITION WORTHY OF A POORLY TRAINED CHIMPANZEE

nice ... nice ... nice
nice ... nice ... nice
nice ... nice ... nice
nice ... nice ... nice

SUBSTITUTES

When you can, find a substitute for a tired word.

Choose more exact adjectives from the box.

1. <u>awful</u> food

2. an <u>awful</u> crime

3. a <u>bad</u> smell

4. a <u>bad</u> accident

5. a <u>boring</u> voice

6. a <u>boring</u> lesson

foul
monotonous
tedious
disgusting
serious
appalling

FIND ANOTHER WORD

Find another word for **got** in each of the sentences below.
Don't use any word more than once.

1. We **got** chocolates for Zelda. _____

2. Colin's **got** a cold. _____

3. We **got** Dad to take us. _____

4. It's **got** very cold. _____

5. We **got** a plumber to mend the leak. _____

6. Steven's **got** a prize! _____

SLANG

There are times when we can use slang and times when we should express ourselves more formally. It's a question of using the kind of language which is right for the situation you're in.

> Yeah, I thought it would go pear-shaped, but then I got well into it as it got blinding. Sorted.

> I anticipated problems, but as matters turned out I found it more and more entertaining – which was very satisfying.

The more words you know, the easier it will be to find the right ones for the occasion.

If you wanted to avoid using these slang expressions, what else could you say?

1. to wind someone up   _____

2. to do your own thing   _____

3. to lose your cool   _____

4. to be conned   _____

5. to be freaked out   _____

ONOMATOPOEIA

Hmm. Tricky word.

Here are some examples of onomatopoeia:

whoosh

squelch

fizz

cuckoo

bubble

crunch

rattle

clatter

splash

ONOMATOPOEIA

What does **onomatopoeia** mean? Well, what do the words on page 25 have in common? Yes, they all sound like the noises they describe.

You've probably used onomatopoeic words before without realising it. You may have talked to a toddler about **baa-lambs** and **moo-cows**. You know that dogs say **woof**, cats **miaow** and ducks **quack**. So there's nothing complicated about onomatopoeia, except the word itself (it comes from two Greek words meaning **name making**). That's all it is – making names to echo sounds.

Think about words that describe the sounds that birds, animals and insects make. Try these:

1. What hisses? _____

2. What buzzes? _____

3. What hoots? _____

4. What screeches? _____

5. What bellows? _____

6. What clucks? _____

7. What gobbles? _____

Now think about sounds in the world around you.

8. What creaks? _____

9. What crackles? _____

10. What slams? _____

11. What sizzles? _____

12. What peals? _____

13. What chugs? _____

A car repaired by Steven

What's the point of all this?

Well, again, you will make more of an impact, be more entertaining, win more friends and arguments, earn more money etc. etc. etc., if you know how to use words. Look:

Good storyteller

I slapped the puck – BLAM! It hissed across the ice and smacked into the goal's backboard: BA-BANG!

Bad storyteller

I briefly applied force to the puck, which progressed across the surface and made firm, noisy contact with the goal structure.

WAYS WITH WORDS

Complete these descriptions of sounds.

1. the rustle of _____

2. the clank of _____

3. the clatter of _____

4. the scrape of _____

5. the smack of _____

6. the pitter-patter of _____

7. the _____ of the wind in the trees

8. the _____ of bare feet on wet concrete

9. the _____ of water in the pipes

10. the _____ of the fluffy little yellow chicks

11. the _____ of thunder overhead

12. the _____ of ice cubes in the glass

Tomorrow morning, before you get up, listen carefully to all the sounds, indoors and out. Make a list, choosing onomatopoeic words to describe them.

The greatest onomatopoeic joke in the history of the world:

1 Have you seen the Brown Paper Cowboy in here?

2 What does he look like?

3 Brown paper hat. Brown paper waistcoat. Brown paper gunbelt.

4 "Brown paper trousers. Brown paper boots. Brown paper spurs."

5 "What's he wanted for?"

And now turn the page for the punchline...

PEOPLE

GROUP WORDS

A collective noun is used to describe a group.
Complete each of these phrases with a collective noun
from the box.
Use a dictionary if you like.

board	gang
regiment	bench
crew	band
company	host

1. a _____ of sailors
2. a _____ of magistrates
3. a _____ of thieves
4. a _____ of angels
5. a _____ of soldiers
6. a _____ of actors
7. a _____ of musicians
8. a _____ of directors

What do you call it when a
boat carrying a fibble of
politicians sinks
to the bottom of the sea?

A good start!

THREE'S A CROWD

What's the difference between a crowd, a rabble and a mob?
They are all large groups of people, but people in different
situations.

crowd	–	a large group of people
rabble	–	a noisy crowd
mob	–	a violent crowd

**A crowd was waiting
for the Queen.**

**A mob was waiting
for the Queen.**

Crowd  **Rabble**  **Crab-apple**

Crabby apple **Rap apple**

Where would you find each of these large groups of people?

1. an audience _____

2. a congregation _____

3. spectators _____

4. a bunch of
   complete losers

CLEVER OR STUPID?

Use words from the Clever Box and the Stupid Box to sum up these people.

1. Mark believes everything he is told.

   Mark is _____.

2. Claire has all the answers.

   Claire is _____.

3. Sarah never considers the consequences of her actions.

   Sarah is _____.

4. Sam never understands jokes.

   Sam is _____.

5. Andy always thinks things through carefully.

   Andy is _____.

6. Zoe is excellent at thinking of ways of solving problems.

   Zoe is _____.

Clever Box	**Stupid Box**
rational	rash
knowledgeable	slow-witted
resourceful	gullible

1 A rash decision

2 Another rash decision

3 A rasher decision

4 Another rasher decision

TRUE OR FALSE?

1. A diligent pupil works very hard. _____

2. An optimistic person always
   expects the worst to happen. _____

3. A thrifty shopper is very extravagant. _____

4. An indolent worker gets a lot done
   in a short time. _____

5. Taciturn people don't say very much. _____

MASCULINE AND FEMININE

Write the female or male equivalent of each of these words.

1. husband   _____
2. uncle   _____
3. monk   _____
4. master   _____
5. prince   _____
6. _____   niece
7. _____   bride
8. _____   widow
9. _____   duchess
10. _____   queen

FIRST NAMES

Some first names can be shortened. However, the full version is often used on formal occasions. Write each of these shortened names in full.

1. Tim   _____
2. Josh   _____
3. Tom   _____
4. Mel   _____
5. Will   _____
6. Sue   _____
7. Ben   _____
8. Jenny   _____

PEOPLE

Write each of these shortened names in full.

9. Pat (girl) _____

10. Pat (boy) _____

11. Jo (girl) _____

12. Joe (boy) _____

13. Sam (girl) _____

14. Sam (boy) _____

15. Charlie (girl) _____

16. Charlie (boy) _____

17. Andy (girl) _____

18. Andy (boy) _____

19. Nicky (girl) _____

20. Nick (boy) _____

OCCUPATIONS

Hi, I'm Tony the Excitable Teacher. My occupation? I'm a teacher!

My job is not just to teach you, but to inspire you to want to learn.

I get to act as a sort of guide, philosopher and friend on your journey to understand ...

... not just facts, but the BEAUTY of WORDS, of KNOWLEDGE ...

... the JOY of SELF-EXPRESSION and UNDERSTANDING ...

... the WONDER of DISCOVERY of the WEALTH that is ... that is ...

I think he's exploded. That's ... er ... bad.

TICK THE RIGHT BOX

Use a dictionary to find out who uses each of these at work.
Tick the box next to each right answer.

STAFF ROOM

It's not me but sometimes I wish it was.

Hack some flesh off for you, sir?

1. **cleaver**
a) teacher ☐
b) hairdresser ☐
c) butcher ☐

2. **baton**
a) conductor of an orchestra ☐
b) bus driver ☐
c) miner ☐

I'm the bus conductor.

3. **scalpel**
a) surgeon ☐
b) fishmonger ☐
c) singer ☐

4. **metronome**
a) pianist ☐
b) nurse ☐
c) architect ☐

Metronomes

Metrognomes

LOST PROPERTY

Give each of these tools back to its owner by drawing a line to connect them. The first one has been done for you.

1. chisel   hairdresser
2. microscope police officer
3. scissors   doctor
4. palette   artist
5. stethoscope carpenter
6. handcuffs   scientist

BRAIN CELL QUESTIONS

Write the missing letters.

USE YOUR DICTIONARY

7. I study rocks.   g__ologist
8. I study birds.   orn__ __ __ologist
9. I study the weather. met__ __ __ologist
10. I study earthquakes. sei__ __ologist

DID YOU KNOW?

It is usually possible to avoid using masculine and feminine job titles. Use the ones that apply to both men and women.

schoolmaster, schoolmistress	–	teacher
headmaster, headmistress	–	head teacher
actor, actress	–	actor
author, authoress	–	author
poet, poetess	–	poet
policeman, policewoman	–	police officer
foreman, forewoman	–	supervisor
spaceman, spacewoman	–	astronaut
male nurse, nurse	–	nurse

Look out for more examples of non-sexist language.

But why? I mean, that's all very politically correct and everything, but why can't I use a perfectly good word like **policemen** to mean both policemen and policewomen? Everyone would know what I meant. What do you say to that?

Get back in the relic cupboard! You're history, loser.

Er, yes. Or you could say that language is a tool, like a tool in a garage. You need it because you want to do things. You want to make your meaning clear. You might want to persuade people. It's probably best to avoid annoying people if you can. And you probably wouldn't want to imply that you think some people are less important than others.

Which of these adverts do you think looks best?

BECOME A POLICEMAN OR A POLICEWOMAN

BECOME A POLICEMAN*
*Please take this word as a reference not just to policemen, but to policewomen, too.

BECOME A POLICE OFFICER

ARE YOU A COLLECTOR?

Do you know these names for collectors?

A person who collects postcards is called a **cartophilist**.

A person who collects coins is called a **numismatist**.

A person who collects stamps is called a **philatelist**.

A person who collects matchboxes is called a **phillumenist**.

THE ANIMAL KINGDOM

Now, I'm not going to on, you or you, but you can have a of a time with words if you don't the same old rubbish until you're .

Don't out — 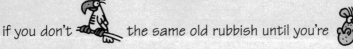 out a new word instead!

That's cooked her .

That's cooked her.

Don't  about it.

ANIMAL HOMES

Match each animal with its home.

1. squirrel _____   lodge
2. badger _____   form
3. beaver _____   warren
4. fox _____   sett

5. hare _____ drey
6. otter _____ earth
7. rabbit _____ holt

Where do these animals sleep?

8. horse _____

9. pig _____

10. cow _____

11. dog _____

12. tame rabbit _____

13. chicken _____

14. bees _____

They all live in here, by the look of it.

JUMBLED LETTERS

Rearrange these letters to spell the name of an eagle's nest.

i y e e r   _ _ _ _ _

DID YOU KNOW?

Canine means **like a dog**.
Feline means **like a cat**.
Equine means **like a horse**.
Bovine means **like a cow**.
Elephantine means **like an elephant**.
Asinine means **like an ass**.

So now you know:

- why our four pointed teeth are called **canines**
- why **elephantine** means **clumsy and ungainly**
- why **feline** grace is beautiful to watch
- why **asinine** behaviour is idiotic
- why **BSE** stands for **Bovine Spongiform Encephalopathy**
- why **equine** studies are connected with horses

**Wino: a person
who likes wine**

**Pino: a person who likes
furniture from IKEA**

GROUPS

What is the group word (collective noun) for each of these animals? Choose the right word from the box.

shoal	flock
swarm	herd
pack	school
litter	

1. bees _____

2. cows _____

3. sheep _____

4. wolves _____

5. whales _____

6. herring _____

7. puppies _____

Complete these phrases. Use a dictionary to help you.

8. a pride of l _ _ _ _
9. a plague of loc _ _ _ _
10. a gaggle of ge _ _ _
11. a brood of ch _ _ _ _ _
12. a covey of part _ _ _ _ _ _ _

An attack of the b_ _ m _ _ sn_ _ m_ _ from F_ _ _ _ _

Here are some very unusual collective nouns. Hardly anyone knows them. Learn the ones you like best – and be a genius!

a **building** of rooks

a **charm** of goldfinches

a **crash** of rhinoceroses

a **murmuration** of starlings

a **muster** of peacocks

a **skein** of geese (in flight)

a **skulk** of foxes

a **watch** of nightingales

a **wisp** of snipe

ANIMAL YOUNG

Unscramble the names of these animal babies.

	Parents			Young
1.	dog	bitch	(upp)	_____
2.	ram	ewe	(blam)	_____
3.	bull	cow	(falc)	_____
4.	stallion	mare	(loaf)	_____
5.	bear	she-bear	(bcu)	_____
6.	billy-goat	nanny-goat	(dki)	_____

DICTIONARY WORK

Complete these phrases. Use a dictionary to help you. Steven has done the first one for you. And got it wrong.

1. A **leveret** is a young _____.

A young lever

2. A **cygnet** is a young _____.

3. A **fawn** is a young _____.

4. A **gosling** is a young _____.

5. An **elver** is a young _____.

6. A **parr** is a young _____.

MATCHMAKING

Pair the animals by choosing words from the box. Your dictionary will help you.

gander	drake	pen
stag	vixen	boar
doe		

	MALE	**FEMALE**
1.	cob (swan)	_____
2.	buck (rabbit)	_____
3.	fox	_____
4.	_____	duck
5.	_____	goose
6.	_____	hind
7.	_____	sow

I called Zelda a foxy chick!

Duck!

Doe!

SMALL OR YOUNG

You can show that something or someone is small or young by using a variety of adjectives.

a **little** boy
a **small** room
a **young** bird
a **tiny** egg
a **miniature** poodle

Another way is to use an ending (suffix).

pig**let**
duck**ling**
kitchen**ette**
hill**ock**

Ah ... no, when I said you were a pillock, I meant you were like a small pill ... er ... something which makes you feel better ...

WHAT AM I?

1. codling   a young   _____
2. sapling   a young   _____
3. driblet   a small   _____
4. rivulet   a small   _____

Give one word for each of these.

5. a young eagle   _____
6. a young goose   _____
7. a very young plant   _____
8. a young owl   _____
9. a very small drop   _____

A very small drop

PICK YOUR OWN

Another way of showing that something is small is to add a prefix such as **mini** or **micro** at the beginning of the word. Using a dictionary, add three more words to each list.

microwave

micro _____

micro _____

micro _____

minibus

mini _____

mini _____

mini _____

Minimum [small mum]

Maximum [large mum]

Minuscule mum [very small mum]

Minischool ... er ... very small school, obviously

AROUND THE WORLD

NATIONALITY ADJECTIVES

How many of these nationality adjectives do you know? The first one has been done for you.

Remember that each one begins with a capital letter, just like the name of the country.

1. Italy   Italian

2. France   _____

3. Greece   _____

4. Norway   _____

5. Spain   _____

6. Poland   _____

7. Iceland   _____

An Italian meal

A French meal

A greasy meal

A meal from Iceland
(Iceland, the shop ... geddit?)

NAME THE COUNTRY

From which country does each of these products come?

1. Dutch tulips   _____

2. Danish bacon   _____

3. Swiss watches   _____

4. Belgian chocolates   _____

5. Turkish coffee   _____

WHERE DO I COME FROM?

It's easy to know where a Scot comes from. He or she comes from Scotland. Unless he's Scott Tracy. Then he comes from Thunderbird Island. But that's a very different issue, and one that we're not dealing with here.

What about these?

1.	I am a Spaniard.	I come from	_____.
2.	I am a Cypriot.	I come from	_____.
3.	I am a Manxman.	I come from	_____.
4.	I am a Finn.	I come from	_____.
5.	I am a Swede.	I come from	_____.
6.	I am a Ghanaian.	I come from	_____.
7.	I am a Chinese.	I come from	_____.

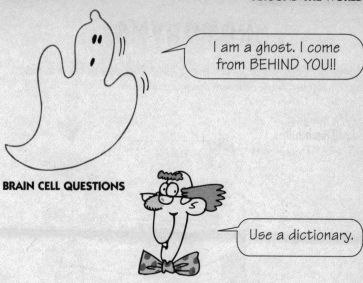

I am a ghost. I come from BEHIND YOU!!

BRAIN CELL QUESTIONS

Use a dictionary.

1. A Breton comes from _____.

2. A Briton comes from _____.

Part Dane, part Swede, part Finn, part Kiwi, Terry usually had a lot of trouble at Customs.

HOMONYMS

Homonyms are words which are spelled and pronounced in the same way but have different meanings.

SAME spelling
SAME sound
DIFFERENT meanings

Zelda has a box of engine parts.

Steven and Colin are trying to box.

Some homonyms have four, five, six or more different meanings.

Let's see how many meanings the word **form** has.

Fill in the **form** in ink.
The team was on top **form**.
Hannah's in the first **form** (Year 7).
Six of you can sit on this **form**.
A hare's home is called a **form**.
I could see a shadowy **form** on the doorstep.
Ice is water in another **form**.
Try to **form** the habit of checking your work before you hand it in.

Can you think of any more?

OVER TO YOU

Which homonyms are illustrated here?

1.

2.

 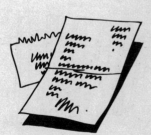

3.

_____

4.

_____

5.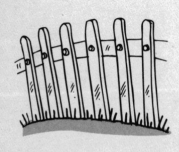

_____

THREES

Each of these words has three meanings. Tick a), b) or c).

1. spring
   a) a plant
   b) coiled wire
   c) a vegetable

   a) a key ring
   b) a kangaroo
   c) a season

   a) to leap into the air
   b) to uncover
   c) to feel happy

2. trunk
   a) a large container for clothes
   b) a cross-channel ferry
   c) an airport

   a) a branch
   b) an extension
   c) the main part of your body

   a) a swimsuit
   b) an elephant's nose
   c) a tall chimney

3. match
   a) a letter
   b) a book
   c) a contest

   a) a lampshade
   b) an impregnated stick which
      produces a flame
   c) a nightmare

   a) to paint something a different colour
   b) to go well with something; to look the same
   c) to take a small cutting from a bush

TEST YOUR WORD POWER

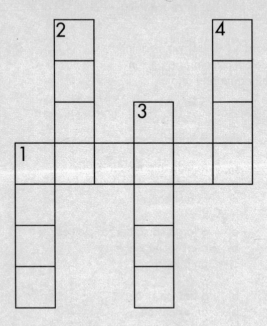

Clues

Across

1. This word has these three meanings:
   - an account, for your parents, of your progress at school
   - a newspaper article about an event
   - a loud bang or explosion

Down

1. This word has these three meanings:
   - a break from work
   - a short sleep
   - what is left over

2. This word has these two meanings:
   - a kind of evergreen tree with cones
   - to miss someone very much

3. This word has these two meanings:
   - a furry layer that grows on old food
   - a container into which liquid is poured and left to harden, taking the shape of the container

4. This word has these two meanings:
   - to defeat a team or a person
   - to hit again and again

Beware of giving someone the wrong impression.

I was late because the coach took the wrong fork and hit the fence.

DICTIONARY WORK

Use a dictionary to help you to find different meanings for each of these words.

1. sound _____ _____

2. coach _____ _____

3. spell _____ _____

_____

4. tie _____ _____

_____

5. hamper _____ _____

A gag can make you laugh ...

... or make you shut up.

HOMOPHONES

Homophones are words which sound alike but are spelled differently and have different meanings.

SAME sound
DIFFERENT spellings
DIFFERENT meanings

Your letter clearly said you wanted a plane design.

PAIRS

Which pairs of homophones fit these definitions? The first one has been done for you.

1. a flat thin piece of wood   board

   not interested at all   bored

2. paper and envelopes   _____

   not moving   _____

3. land at the edge of the sea   _____

   certain   _____

4. to change in some way   _____

   a raised table in a church   _____

MISSING LETTERS

Complete the second homophone of each pair.

1. taught   t __ __ t
2. fate   f __ __ e
3. caught c __ __ __ t

4. medal m __ __ __ __ e
5. profit pr __ __ __ __ t

The fête worse than death

WHICH WORD?

1. My mother _____ me
   the potatoes.   (passed/past)

2. Both kittens _____ very shy. (seam/seem)

3. He doesn't know _____
   he can come.   (weather/whether)

4. Is your dog _____ indoors? (allowed/aloud)

5. His sister is a weekly _____
   at her school.   (boarder/border)

6. The puppy was scared by the
   thunder and _____ . (lightening/lightning)

7. The miser had a _____
   of gold coins.   (hoard/horde)

8. Evan shouted so much that his
   voice was quite _____. (hoarse/horse)

9. I didn't like to say
   that I was _____ by the film. (board/bored)

10. My uncle lives on
    the seventh _____. (storey/story)

LUNCH TIME

Only one of each pair of homophones describes something which can be eaten. Draw a circle round it.

1. currant / current

2. pear / pair

3. stake / steak

4. cereal / serial

BRAIN CELL QUESTIONS

1. **Feet** are on the end of your legs. Agreed?

What is a **feat**? _____

I'm staring de feet in de face.

2. **Dual** means **having two parts**.

What is a duel? _____

But you said I'd be working in a duel capacity.

HOMOGRAPHS

Homographs are words which are spelled in the same way but are pronounced differently and have different meanings.

SAME spelling

DIFFERENT sounds

DIFFERENT meanings

When I saw minute steak on the menu, I thought it would be cooked for a minute. I didn't expect it to be minute!

What did you say about my newt?

Make up two sentences to show the two meanings of this word.

1. perMIT _____

2. PERmit _____

Put all the refuse in the bin right away, and don't you dare to refuse!

Now write the definition for the second word in each pair.

3.   proJECT   to throw your voice

      PROject   _____

4.   preSENT   to give an award or presentation

      PRESent   _____

5.   conDUCT   to control, direct or manage

      CONduct   _____

The Ghost of Christmas presents ... the Ghost of Christmas presents

JUMBLED WORDS

Unscramble these homographs.

1. a) a person who is ill for a long time   nalidiv _____
   b) not legally correct

2. a) the way into a place   tenrncae _____
    b) to delight

COMPUTER TALK

The invention of computers has meant that a lot of new words have had to be devised and old ones adapted.

How computer-literate are you? Let's see!

NERDS' WORDS

These definitions have got muddled up. Can you sort them out?
Draw a line to match each word to its definition.

1. e-mail
a device that makes it possible to send information from one computer to another through the telephone

2. Internet
a large collection of information stored in a computer in such a well organised way that it can easily be found and used

3. database
a network of computers linked by telephone so that people all over the world can get in touch with each other

4. laptop
messages sent by computer

RESEARCH

Use a dictionary to help you to find the origin of some of these terms.

1. e-mail   _ _ _ _ _ _ _ _ _ _ mail
2. Internet inter _ _ _ _ _ _ _ _ net _ _ _ _

What does each of these abbreviations stand for?

3. PC   _____

4. VDU   _____

5. RAM   _____

6. CD-ROM   _____

NEW MEANINGS

They've made surfing so easy — just one click on your mouse and you're on the net.

Write the computer-related definition of each of these words.

1. mouse   a)   a small rodent with a long tail

           b)   _____

                _____

2. window   a)   an opening to let in light and air

           b)   _____

                _____

3. memory   a)   the ability of the mind to recall things

           b)   _____

                _____

4. surf   a)   to ride on a surfboard on big waves in a rough sea

           b)   _____

                _____

BRAIN CELL QUESTION

What is the difference between **outer space** and **cyberspace**?

outer space _____
_____

cyberspace _____
_____

Have you come across the words in this picture?

Peopleware

Into face

Interface

Hardware

Tupperware

MALAPROPISMS

Some people get really mixed up when they use long words. They use ones that sound about right but which have completely the wrong meanings.

Mrs Malaprop is a character in a play called *The Rivals*. She is famous for making mistakes like this. She says **pineapple** when she means **pinnacle**, and **geometry** when she means **geography**. These confusions with words are called **malapropisms** after Mrs Malaprop.

A malapropism can be very funny when someone else says it, but it can be very embarrassing when you're the one who's getting it wrong.

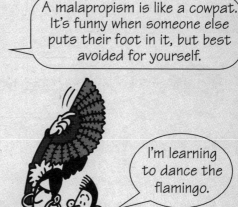

A malapropism is like a cowpat. It's funny when someone else puts their foot in it, but best avoided for yourself.

I'm learning to dance the flamingo.

PUT THESE RIGHT

Cross out the malapropisms and write the correct words underneath.

1. My best friend was <u>adapted</u> when she was eight years old.

    _____

2. We don't have <u>capital</u> punishment in our school any more.

    _____

3. My baby brother is being kept in <u>extensive</u> care at Homerton Hospital.

    _____

4. My grandfather is <u>imperialised</u> from the waist down.

    _____

5. Sally caught the <u>injection</u> from her sister.

    _____

6. My aunt was <u>historical</u> when she heard the news.

    _____

7. I have to have my <u>asteroids</u> out.

    _____

SYNONYMS

Synonyms are words with the same or similar meanings.

Happy: glad, pleased, contented, cheerful

Angry: cross, irritated, annoyed, furious

Remember how helpful thesauruses and dictionaries can be when they're used together.

A dictionary gives the meaning, or meanings, of a word.
A thesaurus lists synonyms for words.

My lord, Timscottus, is ill, unwell, sick, poorly, under the weather ...

The messenger Thesaurus listing symptoms

OVER TO YOU

Find four synonyms for each of these words.

1. obedient _____ _____
   _____ _____

2. delicious _____ _____
   _____ _____

3. horrible _____ _____
   _____ _____

4. cold _____ _____
   _____ _____

SHADES OF MEANING

1   **2**   **3**   **4**   **5**   **6**   **7**

Which marrow is described by each of these words?

tiny _____

gigantic _____

small _____

minute _____

microscopic _____

large _____

huge _____

ODD ONE OUT

Circle the odd one out. Use a dictionary.

1. anxious   apprehensive   jealous   nervous   worried

2. considerate courteous   polite   rich   well-mannered

3. defiant   guilty   rigid   stubborn   unyielding

BRAIN CELL QUESTIONS

You'll probably need a dictionary to help you to explain the difference in meaning between the two words in each pair. See how you get on. Be a genius!

1. gazing   _____
   glancing   _____

2. lending   _____
   borrowing   _____

3. ironing   _____
   pressing   _____

4. cancelling   _____
   postponing   _____

5. complimenting   _____
   flattering   _____

'TALKING' WORDS

Do you know any verbs which describe ways of talking?

... she asked, begged, demanded, requested ...

No one likes a Clevertrousers, you know.

... she said, sneered, spluttered, jeered, moaned, remarked ...

Oh, be quiet.

... she insisted, snapped, bellowed, shrieked ...

Complete these 'talking' words. Read the clues first.

1. wh _ _ _ _ _ _   to speak very quietly
2. _ _ qui _ _   to ask about something
3. m _ _ ble   to mutter or speak unclearly
4. sn _ _ _   to speak nastily like a dog growling
5. y _ _ _   to shout at the top of your voice
6. _ _ _ p   to speak sharply
7. wh _ _ _   to speak in a complaining way

'WALKING' WORDS

Do you know any verbs which describe ways of walking?

I won't say a word this time. I don't want to show off.

SYNONYMS

1. tru _ _ _   to walk wearily with heavy steps
2. l _ _ _   to walk awkwardly with a hurt foot or leg
3. str _ _ _   to walk with long, energetic steps
4. c _ _ _ p   to move very slowly and quietly
5. m _ _ _ _ _   to walk like a soldier on parade
6. pl _ _   to walk slowly and heavily
7. p _ _ _ _ _ to walk in shallow water

ANTONYMS

Antonyms are words which are opposite or very nearly opposite in meaning.

good: bad
rich: poor

Antonym   **Ant on him**

Write an antonym for each of these words.

1. soft   _____

2. fast   _____

3. cold   _____

4. wet   _____

Now try these more difficult ones.

5. admit   d _ _ _

6. increase   de _ _ _ _ _ _

7. attack   de _ _ _ _

8. hope   de _ _ _ _ _

9. build   de _ _ _ _ _ _

A CHANGE FOR THE BETTER

Change Ben's bad school report into a good one by choosing suitable antonyms for the underlined words.

Ben is a very <u>lazy</u> pupil. He <u>never</u> pays attention in class. His work is <u>untidy</u> and his spelling is <u>appalling</u>.

Ben is a very ____ pupil. He ____ pays attention in class. His work is ____ and his spelling is ____.
P.S. This report has not been forged by me.
Love, Ben xxx

PROVERBS

A proverb is a short, wise saying. Most proverbs are several
centuries old.

> Make hay while the sun shines.
>
> We never miss the water until the well runs dry.
>
> A burned child dreads the fire.

Of course, some proverbs are not as useful as they once were.

**She who wears a large bustle
should not bother asking
whether it makes her bum
look big, for obviously it do**

**The other Cro-Magnon man's
axe always seems more flinty**

MATCH THE HALVES

Draw a line to join the two halves of each proverb.
The first one has been done for you.

1.	A rolling stone	will clutch at a straw.
2.	An apple a day	always blames his tools.
3.	A drowning man	saves nine.
4.	One good turn	gathers no moss.
5.	A stitch in time	is an angry man.
6.	A hungry man	deserves another.
7.	A bad workman	keeps the doctor away.

TWO LEVELS OF MEANING

Most proverbs have two levels of meaning: a surface meaning and a more abstract underlying meaning.

For example, the proverb **Make hay while the sun shines** gives good advice to farmers, but it also advises us all to make the most of an opportunity when it comes, because it may not come again.

Give the underlying meaning of each of these three proverbs.

1.   Don't count your chickens before they're hatched.

_____

2.   Look before you leap.

_____

3.   Let sleeping dogs lie.

_____

I was in the original line-up of Westlife, of course, before I became President and married Kate Winslet.

PAIRS

Which proverbs have similar meanings? Copy each of these proverbs under the equivalent one.

> Make hay while the sun shines.
>
> Deeds, not words.
>
> Where there's a will, there's a way.

1. Actions speak louder than words.

    _____

2. If at first you don't succeed, try, try, and try again.

    _____

3. Strike while the iron's hot.

    _____

OPPOSITES

Which proverbs contradict each other? Copy each of these
proverbs under the one it contradicts.

> Too many cooks spoil the broth.
>
> Out of sight, out of mind.
>
> It's never too late to mend.

1. Absence makes the heart grow fonder.

    _____

2. What's done can't be undone.

    _____

3. Many hands make light work.

    _____

WINNING ARGUMENTS WITH PROVERBS

A FREE SELF-HELP COURSE

EXCLUSIVE TO PEOPLE WHO READ THIS PAGE

1. Proverbs have a certain authority. This is probably because people think, "Well, that saying's been around for ages, so there's probably some truth in it."

2. So, if you can come up with a proverb that suits what you're saying, you will instantly get the intellectual advantage in any argument.

3. So, use a proverb to support what you say.

"Come on, Colin, help out – many hands make light work."

"I don't think I should help, Colin. You know what they say – too many cooks spoil the broth."

4. If no proverb is available, make up your own.

Bad parent – tidy room.

PROVERBS FROM OTHER COUNTRIES

These are often similar to our own. Look at these pairs of proverbs.
The first in each pair is Irish and the second is British.

If you lie down with dogs, you'll rise with fleas.
He that touches pitch will be defiled.

One beetle recognises another.
Set a thief to catch a thief.

A trout in the pot is better than a salmon in the sea.
A bird in the hand is worth two in the bush.

A wild goose never reared a tame gosling.
A wild goose never laid a tame egg.

GOVERNMENT DEPARTMENTS THAT DON'T EXIST, NO 32: THE PROVERB-CHECKING DEPARTMENT

PREFIXES

A prefix is a group of letters which can be added at the beginning of a word to change its meaning. Knowing about prefixes can make a lot of words easier to understand.

Yeah. Like you can now understand the word **prefix**.

Er ... not just that, Steven.

Prefix	Origin and meaning	Example
bene	(Latin: **well**)	benefit
fore	(Anglo-Saxon: **before/in front**)	forecast
manu	(Latin: **hand**)	manuscript
psych	(Greek: **mind**)	psychology
tele	(Greek: **afar**)	television
thermo	(Greek: **heat**)	thermometer
trans	(Latin: **across**)	transplant

Now, every time you see one of these prefixes in a word, you'll have a clue to what the word means. For example, you might not know what the word **manuscript** means, but you can break it down into **manu** and **script**. So a manuscript is a piece of writing that has been written by hand, not printed.

OVER TO YOU

Use a prefix from the list above to complete each of these words.

1. _____al — done by hand
2. _____phone — a device for talking to someone in a different place
3. _____name — first name
4. _____iatry — the study and treatment of mental illness
5. _____fuse — to take blood from one person and put it in another
6. _____court — the area in front of a building or petrol station
7. _____factor — someone who gives money, help or support
8. _____stat — a device used to control temperature in equipment

MATCHING UP

Look at the words in the right-hand circle. Give each one a suitable prefix from the left-hand circle, and write the new words.

tri sub
centi anti
circum

marine
cycle
clockwise
navigate
metre

1. _____

2. _____

3. _____

4. _____

5. _____

DETECTIVE WORK

What does each of these prefixes mean? The first one has been solved for you.

1. decade   decimal   decathlon

   dec means **ten**

2. bicycle   bisect   bifocals

   bi means _____

3. postpone   postscript post-mortem

   post means _____

Clue: If you're waiting for something through the post, it usually arrives after it should.

4. expel   export   extract

   ex means _____

5. contradict   contrary   contrast

   contra means _____

6. international   intervene   interactive

   inter means _____

NEGATIVE PREFIXES

Four prefixes can give some words the opposite in meaning:

	in	**un**	**dis**	**mis**
visible	**in**visible			
happy	**un**happy			
appear	**dis**appear			
behave	**mis**behave			

Spelling tip 1

Remember that you may end up with a double letter.

un + natural	**un**natural
dis + satisfied	**dis**satisfied
mis + spelled	**mis**spelled

Spelling tip 2

Notice that the prefix **in** can change to **il**, **im** or **ir**, to make the word easier to say.

legal	**il**legal
mortal	**im**mortal
possible	**im**possible
regular	**ir**regular

Use **in**, **un**, **dis** or **mis** to make each of these words opposite in meaning.

1. ___real
2. ___honest
3. ___obey
4. ___credible
5. ___advantage
6. ___accurate
7. ___fortune
8. ___equal

Oh, Suzie, you're impossible!

SPELLING TEST

Complete each of these prefixed words.

Use a dictionary.

PREFIXES

1. i _ mature
2. i _ resistible
3. i _ literate
4. i _ logical
5. i _ capable
6. i _ patient

These spellings are tricky, but they show once again that you've just got to know your words. And not just because if you write that a person is **inliterate**, someone may write the same thing about you!

The real reason is that if you get a word wrong, you might end up saying something you don't really mean.

I want to get Toby chocolates because he is an in-patient.

I want to get Toby chocolates because he is impatient.

SUFFIXES

Suffix is an English county next to Norfix, where trousers are free and people build huge raspberry hills to ward off evil hats.

A suffix is a group of syllables which can be added at the end of a word to change its meaning.

care	+	ful	care**ful**
king	+	dom	king**dom**
profit	+	able	profit**able**
sweet	+	ness	sweet**ness**

OVER TO YOU

al   ous   some   able   less

Use one of the above suffixes to complete each of these words.
Use each suffix once only.

1. help_____

2. comfort_____

3. quarrel_____

4. accident_____

5. danger_____

Now try these.

ment   ness   ism   hood   ship

6. child_____

7. disappoint_____

8. owner_____

9. hero_____

10. late_____

SPELLING TEST

Some pairs of suffixes are difficult to spell because they sound the same. Rewrite each of these suffixed words, using the correctly spelled suffix. Use a dictionary if you wish.

1. intelligant   intelligent   _____

2. visable   visible   _____

3. beggar   begger   _____

4. conducter   conductor   _____

5. necessary necessery _____
6. unbelievable unbelievible _____

FIRST AID

Help! Can you correct each of the nouns that Steven has spelled wrongly?

		Steven's go	Your go
1.	angry	angriness	_____
2.	envious	enviousness	_____
3.	honest	honestness	_____
4.	loyal	loyalness	_____
5.	sober	soberness	_____
6.	wise	wiseness	_____

SIMILES

Similes are like ...
cool, man.

A simile is a way of comparing one thing with another.
Most similes begin with **like** or **as**.

Like, "I like you."

No, not like that.
Like this: Zelda's
voice was like
thunder.

Steven's brain
was as sharp
as porridge.

Complete these well known similes.

1. as cool as a _____

2. as dry as a _____

3. as warm as _____

4. to run like the _____

5. to tremble like a _____

6. to sink like a _____

Write the missing words.

7. as _____ as an eel

8. as _____ as a mule

9. as _____ as a peacock

10. as _____ as snow

11. as _____ as ice

12. as _____ as a feather

These similes are fine in conversation, but it's always best to make up your own when you are writing a story or a description. Your own carefully chosen similes will be more vivid and exciting.

OVER TO YOU

Think of good ways of completing these similes.

1. as soft as _____

2. as helpless as _____

3. as contented as _____

4. as stubborn as _____

FILL THE BLANKS

A new short story for Radio Simile

Nicky and Simon stopped suddenly.

"Did you hear that?" Simon whispered.

"Yes," breathed Nicky, her face as white as _____ and her heart pounding in her chest like _____.

"We've got to get back to the village. We've got to get help. We've got to run like _____ but be as quiet as _____. Come on!"

YOU CHOOSE

Look at these comparisons. Underline the ones you like best, and try to explain the reasons for your choices.

1. as plump as   a cabbage
                   a chicken
                   a cushion

_____

2. as thick as   a parrot
                 a brick
                 Mum's gravy

_____

3. as quick as   greased lightning
                 tigers in a hurry
                 a short flash

_____

IDIOMS

An idiom is an expression used in everyday conversation. An idiom is not meant to be taken literally!

to be over the moon	=	to be delighted
to rain cats and dogs	=	to rain heavily
to burn the candle at both ends	=	to overdo work and play
to sit on the fence	=	to avoid taking sides

I'm not **over the moon** about the result. Maybe it was because our goalkeeper has been **burning the candle at both ends**. Maybe it was because it was **raining cats and dogs**. I'll **sit on the fence**. But the **bottom line** is that we lost 67-0.

Stupid idiom!

OVER TO YOU

Explain what each of these expressions means.

1. to sweep something under the carpet

_____

2. to bottle up your feelings

_____

3. to have your heart in your mouth

_____

MATCH THEM UP

Choose the correct meaning for each of these idioms. Write the letters in the boxes.

1. to put the cart before the horse ☐

2. to smell a rat ☐

3. to put the cat among the pigeons ☐

4. to take the bull by the horns ☐

5. to act the goat ☐

a) to be suspicious

b) to act foolishly

c) to stir up trouble

d) to act boldly

e) to do things the wrong way round

WHICH BIT?

Circle the right body part!

1. to be very busy   to be up to one's (mouth   neck   eyes)

2. to listen with
    rapt attention   to be all (hair   ears   nose)

3. to be miserable   to be down in the (toes   nose   mouth)

4. to spoil something   to put your (foot   intestines
                                                        eyeball)   in it

5. to be silent   to hold your (knee   tongue   jugular)

EPONYMS

The word **eponym** comes from two Greek words meaning **named on**. Eponyms are the people after whom things have been named.

Biro: a ballpoint pen invented by Lazlo Jozsef Biro; it first went on sale in 1938

Hoover: a vacuum cleaner manufactured by William Henry Hoover in 1908

Sandwich: a snack made popular by John Montagu, 4th Earl of Sandwich, who resented wasting good gambling time by stopping for a sit-down meal

WHAT AM I?

1. I am a warm knitted jacket, first worn by soldiers led by
    Lord Cardigan in the Crimean War.

    I am a _____.

2. I am a unit that measures the force of an electric current.
    I was devised by the man who invented the first electric
    battery, Alessandro Volta.

    I am a _____.

3. I am a waterproof raincoat developed and manufactured by
    the Scottish chemist, Charles Macintosh.

    I am a _____.

4. I am a kind of mechanical digger, first manufactured
    by J C Bamford.

    I am a _____.

FLOWER POWER

Each of these flowers was named to honour a person who was famous in his own field of study. Match the flowers with the people they were named after.

aubretia   **dahlia**   **fuchsia**   **gardenia**   **buddleia**

1. Leonhard Fuchs (1501 – 66)   German botanist _____

2. Andreas Dahl (1751– 89)   Swedish botanist _____

3. Alexander Garden (1730 – 91) Scottish naturalist _____

4. Claude Aubriet (1668 – 1743) French painter _____

5. Adam Buddle (died 1715)   English botanist _____

Terry Timetraveller (1964 – 1701) The plant which grew backwards in time

DID YOU KNOW?

Nike ® sportswear is named (appropriately) after Nike, the Greek goddess of victory.

Lego ® is not named after a person; the name comes from the Danish **leg godt** meaning **play well**.

Adidas ® sportswear takes its name from Adolf (Adi) Dassler who founded his business in Germany in 1948.

DIALECT WORDS

Many words that might otherwise have passed out of the language have survived as local dialects in different parts of the British Isles.

For example, in one place people might say **daps**, not **plimsolls**.

Is that the same as **gymshoes**?

Yes.

Do you mean **trainers**?

Yes, yes, do let's get on.

The point is, you might need to be careful because ...

LOOK OUT!

... a word might mean one thing in one place, but something quite different in another place.

For example, if someone says they are **putting their pumps on**, they probably aren't doing this ...

DIALECT WORDS

Many dictionaries include dialect words. They are usually indicated by the word **dialect** in brackets.

Don't worry if you can't find all the following dialect words in your dictionary. See how many meanings you can guess correctly, and then look at the answers in the back of the book.

daps	passage	brook
maid	weans	sandshoes
elevenses	bait	snap
bairns	beck	childer
burn	pumps	alley
lassie	ferntickles	snicket

Now find some dialect words in the box for each of the following.

1. stream   _____ _____ _____

2. trainers   _____ _____ _____

3. freckles   _____

4. girl   _____ _____

5. back lane   _____ _____ _____

6. packed lunch   _____ _____ _____

7. children   _____ _____ _____

WORDS THAT HAVE DIED

Some of the words your grandparents and great-grandparents use may seem very old-fashioned to you. You probably understand them but you wouldn't use them yourself.

TRANSLATE 1

What is the modern equivalent of each of these words? There's a clue for the first one.

1. spectacles _____

Clue: He's making a spectacle of himself.

2. charabanc _____

3. wireless _____

4. gramophone _____

5. shilling _____

6. frock _____

Why do I need to know about these words?

There are two reasons:

1 So you can understand what you read

2 So you can mock old people with a keener savagery

For example:

Listen, if you don't like it, Grandad, just get back on your charabanc, go home and listen to some nice Jim Reeves song with your ear trumpet.

TRANSLATE 2

The language in the left-hand sentences goes back even further in time. The phrases on the right are the modern slang equivalents. Write reasonable modern English versions in the spaces.

1. How dost thou?

   Wasssssssaaaaaaaaa!

   _____

2. Wilt thou have this woman to thy lawful wedded wife?

   You fancy her, or wha'?

   _____

3. Prithee, come with me thither.

   Oi, over there!

   _____

4. As thou hast done, so be it done unto you.

   Same to you with knobs on.

   _____

5. Judge not that ye be not judged.

   Coming from you ...

   _____

6. Looke ere ye leape.

   Doh!

   _____

IN A NUTSHELL

If you have a wide vocabulary, you can often use a word or a phrase instead of a long list or a roundabout way of saying something, so you don't just end up banging on and on about the same thing without really adding much to what you're saying except a very real sense of boredom and almost certainly bewilderment in the ears of your listener or the eyes of your reader, whichever is appropriate, the point being that people can only take in so much at any one time, and so often it's better to be brief and to the point — otherwise known as being concise.

Or to put it another way:

If you know the right words
you can be concise.
That makes for clearer,
easier reading, and more impact.

CLASSIFICATION

Sum up each of these lists with a single word.

1. hammer, screwdriver, chisel, pliers, spanner _____
2. beans, cabbage, sprouts, onions, carrots _____
3. copper, zinc, lead, aluminium, tin _____
4. robin, starling, magpie, thrush, swallow _____
5. French, German, Gaelic, Italian, Spanish _____
6. plates, bowls, mugs, cups, saucers _____
7. dahlia, marigold, pansy, geranium, hollyhock _____
8. football, hockey, tennis, netball, basketball _____
9. shield, lance, bayonet, gun, dagger _____
10. mackerel, skate, haddock, cod, tuna _____

BEING CONCISE

Rewrite these sentences more concisely, trying to keep to the number of words in the brackets at the end of each sentence.

1. The millionaire hoarded diamonds, emeralds, rubies and sapphires. (5)

   _____

2. I helped my grandmother polish the forks, knives and spoons. (7)

   _____

3. Only drinks like cola, orange juice and lemonade will be served at the disco. (9)

   _____

4. Class 6 volunteered to collect all the empty crisp packets, sweet wrappers, cigarette ends, drinks cans, paper bags and stuff like that. (8)

_____

5. Sean has two cats, a dog, a hamster, five guinea-pigs and a rabbit. (4)

_____

ONE WORD

Find one word to replace each definition.

1. Something you write or say to admit that you're sorry a_____

2. An act that is against the law c_____

3. A dangerous situation which needs immediate action e_____

4. A heated discussion between people who disagree about something a_____

5. A feeling of annoyance and envy because someone has something or has achieved something that you haven't i_____

IN A NUTSHELL

Replace each group of underlined words with one word. Steven
has done two of them already. Unfortunately, he got them wrong.

6. My friend is a <u>person who never eats meat</u>.

   My friend is a v_____.

Vulcan.

7. Mr. and Mrs. Weston have decided to <u>leave Britain and
   move permanently</u> to Australia.

   Mr. and Mrs. Weston have decided to e_____
   to Australia.

8. I am trying not to be so <u>wasteful with money</u>.
   I am trying not to be so e_____.

9. Didn't you realise that Rosa was a <u>child whose parents
   are dead</u>?

   Didn't you realise that Rosa was an o_____?

10. You need to rest and to eat sensibly when you are <u>recovering
    from an illness</u>.

    You need to rest and to eat sensibly when you
    are c_____.

Chicken Licken.

114

ANSWERS

WORD ROOTS (P11)

1. pedal
2. pedestrian
3. pedicure
4. centipede
5. arranged in the order in which things happened
6. to make two or more things happen at the same time
7. long-lasting
8. a watch or clock which measures time exactly
9. able to be read
10. a tall stand which holds a speaker's notes
11. a formal talk which teaches or gives information
12. (not from the Latin **legere**)
13. Hypothermia is a condition in which the body temperature becomes too low – below the heat level required for survival.

Dictionary Search 1

1. becoming an adult
2. becoming healthy
3. becoming fizzy
4. becoming obsolete
5. becoming rotten

Dictionary Search 2

(suggestions)

technical
technicality
technician
technique
technology
novel
novelty
novice

dynamic
dynamics
dynamite
dynamo
magnanimous
magnate
magnify
magnitude

BORROWED WORDS (P16)

Food and drink

1. Italian
2. Arabic
3. French
4. Hindi
5. Arabic
6. French
7. Russian

Word search

1. courgette
2. curry
3. brochure
4. yoga
5. café
6. polo
7. wigwam
8. siesta
9. encore
10. oboe

Foreign phrases

1. a no-through road /a short road blocked at one end
2. with a bathroom leading off
3. for every year
4. (exchange of services) usually a young person from overseas who will do

ANSWERS

light housework and look after children in exchange for food, accommodation and pocket money
5. the other way round
6. Please reply.

What am I?
1. alligator
2. shampoo
3. robot
4. giraffe
5. khaki
6. bangle

OVERUSED WORDS (P21)
Over to you
1. honest, thoughtful, kind, helpful
2. talented, tuneful, rhythmic, entertaining
3. delicious, tasty, appetising, satisfying

Substitutes
1. disgusting
2. appalling
3. foul
4. serious
5. monotonous
6. tedious

Find another word
(suggestions)
1. bought
2. caught
3. persuaded
4. become
5. found
6. won

Slang
1. to tease someone until he/she becomes annoyed or anxious

2. to do what you want to do and pay no attention to other people
3. to lose your self-control
4. to be tricked or deceived
5. to behave hysterically

ONOMATOPOEIA (P25)
1. a snake
2. a bee
3. an owl
4. a peacock
5. a bull
6. a hen
7. a turkey
8. a door/stairs/a chair
9. wood burning/dry leaves
10. a door
11. something frying
12. a bell
13. a boat engine

Ways with words
(suggestions)
1. silk/leaves in the breeze
2. chains
3. hoofs/china
4. chalk on a blackboard
5. water against a boat/ a ball against a bat
6. raindrops/tiny feet
7. moaning/sighing/sobbing
8. slap
9. gurgling
10. cheeping
11. crash/rumble
12. tinkling

PEOPLE (P31)
Group words
1. crew
2. bench

3. gang
4. host
5. regiment
6. company
7. band
8. board

Three's a crowd
1. theatre
2. church
3. match

Clever or stupid?
1. gullible
2. knowledgeable
3. rash
4. slow-witted
5. rational
6. resourceful

True or false?
1. true
2. false
3. false
4. false
5. true

Masculine and feminine
1. wife
2. aunt
3. nun
4. mistress
5. princess
6. nephew
7. groom
8. widower
9. duke
10. king

First names
1. Timothy
2. Joshua
3. Thomas
4. Melanie
5. William
6. Susan
7. Benjamin
8. Jennifer
9. Patricia
10. Patrick
11. Josephine, Joanne or Joanna
12. Joseph
13. Samantha
14. Samuel
15. Charlotte
16. Charles
17. Andrea
18. Andrew
19. Nicola
20. Nicholas

OCCUPATIONS (P37)
Tick the right box
1. c
2. a
3. a
4. a

Lost property
1. carpenter
2. scientist
3. hairdresser
4. artist
5. doctor
6. police officer

Brain cell questions
1. geologist
2. ornithologist
3. meteorologist
4. seismologist

THE ANIMAL KINGDOM (P42)
1. rabbit
2. badger
3. boar (bore)
4. whale
5. parrot
6. horse (hoarse)

7. chicken
8. fish
9. goose
10. crow

Animal homes

1. drey
2. sett
3. lodge
4. earth
5. form
6. holt
7. warren
8. stable
9. sty
10. byre/cowshed
11. kennel
12. hutch
13. coop/henhouse
14. hive

Jumbled letters

eyrie

Groups

1. swarm
2. herd
3. flock
4. pack
5. school
6. shoal
7. litter
8. lions
9. locusts
10. geese
11. chicks
12. partridges

An attack of the big mad snowmen from France

Animal young

1. pup
2. lamb
3. calf
4. foal
5. cub
6. kid

Dictionary work

1. hare
2. swan
3. deer
4. goose
5. eel
6. salmon

Matchmaking

1. pen
2. doe
3. vixen
4. drake
5. gander
6. stag
7. boar

SMALL OR YOUNG (P48)
What am I?

1. cod
2. tree
3. amount/drop/trickle
4. stream
5. eaglet
6. gosling
7. seedling
8. owlet
9. droplet

Pick your own
(suggestions)

microbe, microchip, microfilm, microlight, microphone, microprocessor, microscope, microsurgery; miniskirt, miniature, minimal, minimum

AROUND THE WORLD (P51)
Nationality adjectives

1. Italian

2. French
3. Greek
4. Norwegian
5. Spanish
6. Polish
7. Icelandic

Name the country
1. Holland
2. Denmark
3. Switzerland
4. Belgium
5. Turkey

Where do I come from?
1. Spain
2. Cyprus
3. The Isle of Man
4. Finland
5. Sweden
6. Ghana
7. China

Brain cell questions
1. Brittany
2. Great Britain

HOMONYMS (P54)
Over to you
1. bulb
2. letter
3. wave
4. fork
5. fence/fencing

Threes
1. b, c, a
2. a, c, b
3. c, b, b

2. TEST YOUR WORD POWER
1. (across)   report
1. (down)   rest
2. (down)   pine
3. (down)   mould
4. (down)   beat

Dictionary work
1. a noise, healthy
2. a bus, to train or teach
3. to use the right letters, magic words, a short period of time
4. to fasten, to score equally, a narrow piece of cloth worn around the neck
5. to hinder, a large basket

HOMOPHONES (P61)
Pairs
1. board, bored
2. stationery, stationary
3. shore, sure
4. alter, altar

Missing letters
1. taut
2. fête
3. court
4. meddle
5. prophet

Which word?
1. passed
2. seem
3. whether
4. allowed
5. boarder
6. lightning
7. hoard
8. hoarse
9. bored
10. storey

Lunch time
1. currant
2. pear
3. steak
4. cereal

Brain cell questions
1. a remarkable achievement

2. an arranged fight between two people using weapons

HOMOGRAPHS (P65)

1. *a sentence in which **permit** means **allow***
2. *a sentence in which **permit** means **a special pass***
3. a special piece of work involving research
4. a gift
5. behaviour

Jumbled words

1. invalid
2. entrance

COMPUTER TALK (P69)
Nerds' words

1. messages sent by computer
2. a network of computers linked by telephone so that people all over the world can get in touch with each other
3. a large collection of information stored in a computer in such a well organised way that it can easily be found and used
4. a small portable computer

Research

1. electronic mail
2. international network
3. personal computer
4. visual display unit
5. random access memory
6. compact disc (read-only memory)

New meanings

1. a device which enables you to move the cursor on a computer screen
2. a window-shaped space on a computer screen which can be controlled separately
3. the part of a computer where information is stored
4. to explore the Internet

Brain cell question

Outer space lies beyond the Earth's atmosphere.
Cyberspace is the name given to the electronic world in which people can communicate on the Internet.

MALAPROPISMS (P73)
Put these right

1. adopted
2. corporal
3. intensive
4. paralysed
5. infection
6. hysterical
7. adenoids

SYNONYMS (P75)
Over to you
(suggestions)

1. disciplined, well-behaved, dutiful, good, law-abiding, docile

2. appetising, tasty, luscious, delectable, pleasant, palatable, scrumptious
3. gross, terrible, horrific, nasty, beastly, ghastly, horrid, awful
4. chilly, bitter, freezing, icy, arctic, biting, wintry (temperature); callous, unfeeling, insensitive, hard-hearted, unfeeling (feelings)

Shades of meaning
3, 7, 4, 2, 1, 5, 6

Odd one out
1. jealous
2. rich
3. guilty

Brain cell questions
1. gazing – looking fixedly
   glancing – looking briefly
2. lending – loaning something to someone
   borrowing – accepting something for temporary use
3. ironing – passing an iron over cloth to remove creases
   pressing – applying pressure with a hot iron (often using a damp cloth as well)
4. cancelling – calling off or stopping
   postponing – putting off to a later date
5. complimenting – praising genuinely
   flattering – saying nice things that aren't true

'Talking' words
1. whisper
2. enquire
3. mumble
4. snarl
5. yell
6. snap
7. whine

'Walking' words
1. trudge
2. limp
3. stride
4. creep
5. march
6. plod
7. paddle

ANTONYMS (P81)
1. hard
2. slow
3. hot
4. dry
5. deny
6. decrease
7. defend
8. despair
9. demolish

A change for the better
hardworking/diligent/conscientious; always; neat; excellent/pleasing/wonderful

PROVERBS (P83)
Match the halves
1. gathers no moss.
2. keeps the doctor away.
3. will clutch at a straw.
4. deserves another.
5. saves nine.
6. is an angry man.
7. always blames his tools.

Two levels of meaning
1. Don't be over-optimistic.

Things can go wrong.
2. Think carefully before you do anything.
3. Don't do anything that will cause unnecessary trouble.

Pairs
1. Deeds, not words.
2. Where there's a will, there's a way.
3. Make hay while the sun shines.

Opposites
1. Out of sight, out of mind.
2. It's never too late to mend.
3. Too many cooks spoil the broth.

PREFIXES (P88)
Over to you
1. manual
2. telephone
3. forename
4. psychiatry
5. transfuse
6. forecourt
7. benefactor
8. thermostat

Matching up
1. tricycle
2. submarine
3. centimetre
4. anticlockwise
5. circumnavigate

Detective work
1. **dec** means **ten**
2. **bi** means **two**
3. **post** means **after**
4. **ex** means **out of**
5. **contra** means **against**
6. **inter** means **between**

Negative prefixes
1. unreal
2. dishonest
3. disobey
4. incredible
5. disadvantage
6. inaccurate
7. misfortune
8. unequal

Spelling test
1. immature
2. irresistible
3. illiterate
4. illogical
5. incapable
6. impatient

SUFFIXES (P95)
Over to you
1. helpless
2. comfortable
3. quarrelsome
4. accidental
5. dangerous
6. childhood
7. disappointment
8. ownership
9. heroism
10. lateness

Spelling test
1. intelligent
2. visible
3. beggar
4. conductor
5. necessary
6. unbelievable

First aid
1. anger
2. envy
3. honesty
4. loyalty

5. sobriety
6. wisdom

SIMILES (P98)
1. cucumber
2. bone
3. toast
4. wind
5. leaf
6. stone
7. slippery
8. obstinate/stubborn
9. proud
10. white
11. cold
12. light

Over to you
Own choice
Fill the blanks
Own choice
You choose
Own choice

IDIOMS (P101)
Over to you
1. to ignore a problem by hoping it will be forgotten
2. to hide what you're really feeling
3. to be very nervous and apprehensive

Match them up
1.e 2.a 3.c 4.d 5.b

Which bit?
1. eyes
2. ears
3. mouth
4. foot
5. tongue

EPONYMS (P104)
What am I?
1. cardigan
2. volt
3. macintosh
4. JCB

Flower power
1. fuchsia
2. dahlia
3. gardenia
4. aubretia
5. buddleia

DIALECT WORDS (P107)
1. burn, beck, brook
2. daps, pumps, sandshoes
3. ferntickles
4. maid, lassie
5. passage, alley, snicket
6. elevenses, bait, snap
7. bairns, weans, childer

WORDS THAT HAVE DIED (P109)
Translate 1
1. glasses
2. coach
3. radio
4. CD player
5. 5p
6. dress

Translate 2
(along these lines)
1. How are you?
2. Do you agree to marry this woman?
3. Please go over there with me.
4. You deserve to be treated by others exactly as you've treated them in the past.
5. Never criticise others or

they'll criticise you.
6. Look before you leap.

IN A NUTSHELL (P111)
Classification
1. tools
2. vegetables
3. metals
4. birds
5. languages
6. crockery/china
7. flowers
8. games/sports
9. weapons
10. fish

Being concise
1. The millionaire hoarded precious gems.
2. I helped my grandmother polish the cutlery/silver.
3. Only soft drinks will be served at the disco.
4. Class 6 volunteered to collect all the litter/rubbish.
5. Sean has ten pets.

One word
1. apology
2. crime
3. emergency
4. argument
5. jealousy
6. vegetarian
7. emigrate
8. extravagant
9. orphan
10. convalescent/convalescing

ORDER FORM

0 340 89336 2	Grammar Repair Kit	£4.99	☐
0 340 89334 6	Punctuation Repair Kit	£4.99	☐
0 340 89335 4	Spelling Repair Kit	£4.99	☐
0 340 91835 7	Maths Repair Kit	£4.99	☐
0 340 91833 0	Science Repair Kit	£4.99	☐

Books in this series are available at your local bookshop, or can be ordered direct from the publisher. A complete list of titles is given above. Just tick the titles you would like and complete the details below. Prices and availability are subject to change without prior notice.

Please enclose a cheque or postal order made payable to Bookpoint Ltd, and send to: Hodder Children's Books, Cash Sales Dept, Bookpoint, 130 Milton Park, Abingdon, Oxon OX14 4SB. Email address: UK.orders@bookpoint.co.uk.

If you would prefer to pay by credit card, our call centre team would be delighted to take your order by telephone. Our direct line is 01235 400414 (lines open 9.00 am – 5.00 pm, Monday to Friday; 24 hour message answering service). Alternatively you can send a fax on 01235 400454.

Title .... First name .... Surname ....

Address..

....

....

Daytime tel .... Postcode ....

If you would prefer to post a credit card order, please complete the following.

Please debit my Visa/Access/Diners Card/American Express (delete as applicable) card number:

Signature .... Expiry Date ....

If you would NOT like to receive further information on our products, please tick ☐.